FUN FACTS

Ripley's
Believe It or Not!®
Kids

& SILLY STORIES

6

Project Editor Jordie R. Orlando
Designers Luis Fuentes, Penny Stamp
Reprographics *POST LLC

ISBN 978-1-60991-183-6 (US)

Library of Congress Control Number: 2017936859

For information regarding permission, write to
VP Intellectual Property
Ripley Entertainment Inc.
Suite 188, 7576 Kingspointe Parkway
Orlando, Florida, 32819
publishing@ripleys.com
www.ripleybooks.com

Manufactured in China
in June/2017
1st printing

PUBLISHER'S NOTE
While every effort has been made to verify the accuracy
of the entries in this book, the Publishers cannot be held
responsible for any errors contained in the work. They
would be glad to receive any information from readers.

WARNING
Some of the stunts and activities in this book are undertaken
by experts and should not be attempted by anyone without
adequate training and supervision.

a Jim Pattison Company

FUN FACTS

Ripley's
Believe It or Not!®
Kids

& SILLY STORIES

6

A photographer snapped photos of **penguins** leaping out of the water to make it look like they're surfing!

One of the largest icebergs ever recorded was bigger than the island of Jamaica.

Bees can be trained to find EXPLOSIVES.

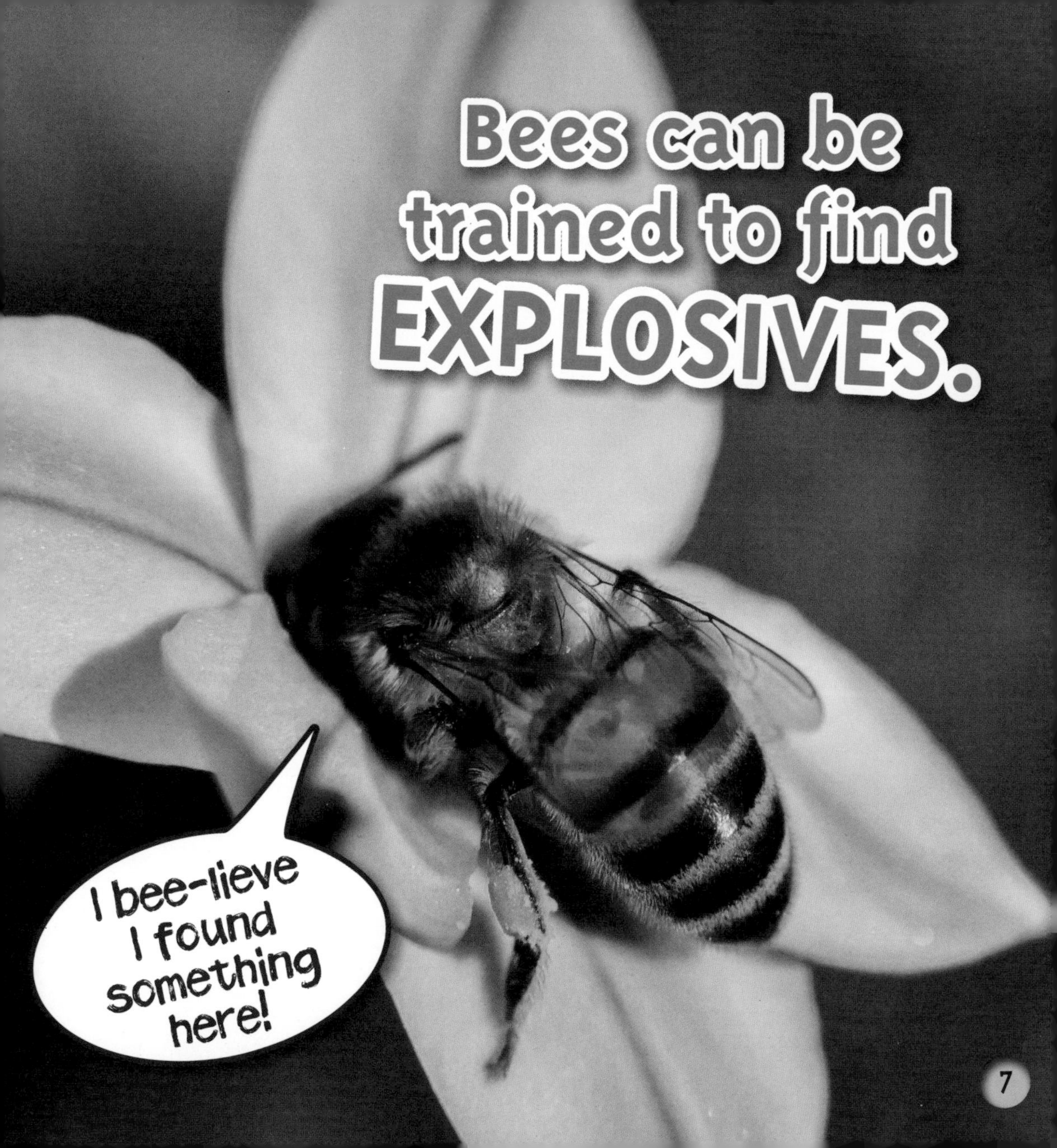

The PlayStation® 1 controller was slightly larger in the U.S. than in Japan because Americans have larger hands.

Cats can become ADDICTED to tuna.

There are more venomous fish in the world (over 1,200 species) than there are venomous snakes!

GO-GO Gorillas

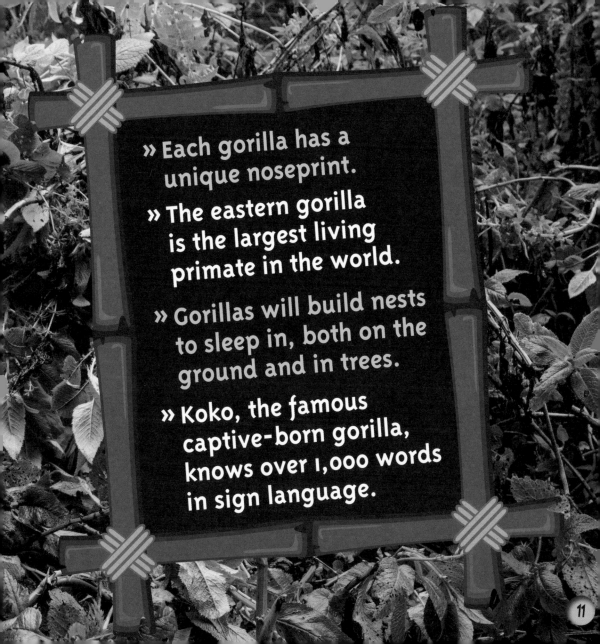

» Each gorilla has a unique noseprint.

» The eastern gorilla is the largest living primate in the world.

» Gorillas will build nests to sleep in, both on the ground and in trees.

» Koko, the famous captive-born gorilla, knows over 1,000 words in sign language.

A healthy adult can have 6 pounds (2.7 kg) of microorganisms living in their body!

There is a species of beetle that rides ants.

A pelican's mouth

can hold more than its stomach.

Strong **EARTHQUAKES** can make the Earth spin faster.

Pumpkin Spice flavoring can be made up of more than 300 ingredients, but no pumpkin.

A mall in Shanghai, China, has a slide

that's five stories tall!

In Rhode Island, you cannot dye

a duckling, a chick, or other live poultry.

19

The French version of LOL is MDR, short for **mort de rire,** or "dying of laughter."

MDR!

Crabs have teeth in their stomachs.

Some people never develop fingerprints.

The *Harry Potter* books have been translated into nearly 70 languages.

A young eel is called an elver.

SPACE FACTS

The sun rises only twice a year on Venus.

The Apollo astronauts' footprints could remain on the Moon for millions of years!

If two pieces of the same type of metal touch in the vacuum of space, they will stick together permanently.

Sound waves cannot travel through space.

A reptile breeder in Georgia produced a ball python with a smiley face pattern!

Some eucalyptus trees contain small amounts of GOLD.

Paper money is not made of paper.

Put your wings together!

Chickens star in the **Hens and Friends** charity calendar series, created by Teresa Delcambre of Commerce, Texas.

She dresses up her 60 chickens in costumes like Elvis, Santa Claus, and Dracula!

Hawaii's state fish is the **humuhumunukunukuapua'a** (also known as the reef trigger fish).

Donkeys living on the French island Île de Ré wear pants to protect their legs from bugs!

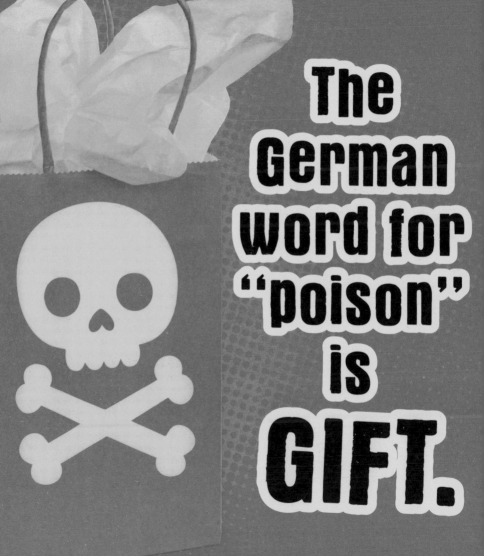

The German word for "poison" is GIFT.

It would take 225 million years to walk the distance light travels in a year.

Biologists in the Netherlands created a dating app for orangutans.

Antarctica is the largest desert on Earth.

Campanology is the art of bell ringing.

President Ronald Reagan's Secret Service code name was "Rawhide."

Who would EMU-gine that!

Emus can't walk backwards.

SCRAPPY THE CAT'S

UNIQUE BLACK AND WHITE FUR EARNED HIM OVER 100,000 FOLLOWERS ON INSTAGRAM.

These four Boston Terriers living in Scotland dressed the part when their owner found children's kilts that fit them perfectly.

43

The UNICORN

is Scotland's national animal.

English artist Cléon Daniel created this doughnut-shaped pool table!

Dr. Seuss's *Green Eggs and Ham* was the result of a challenge to write a book with exactly 50 unique words.

Some countries race camels with **robot jockeys!**

A city Councilman in San Jose, California, was sworn in on Captain America's shield.

Larry the Cat

is the Chief Mouser to the Cabinet Office of the United Kingdom and is responsible for keeping rodents out of government headquarters!

GEESE
have serrated tongues.

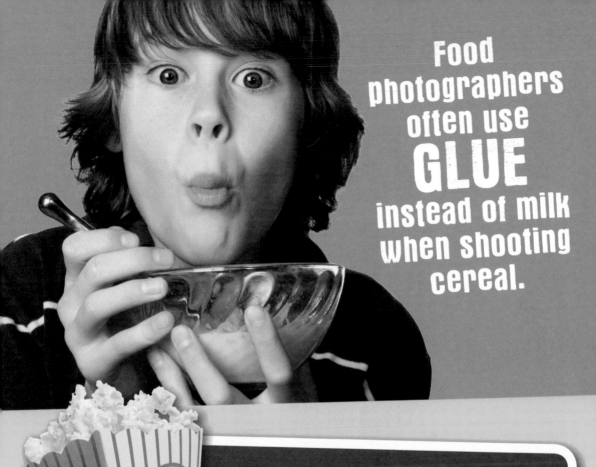

Food photographers often use **GLUE** instead of milk when shooting cereal.

People eat 28 percent more popcorn while watching sad movies.

A cow in China grew **A THIRD HORN** in the middle of its head!

BULL-ieve It or Not!

You can eat dinner underwater inside "The Pearl" in Brussels, Belgium.

Elephants use sand to protect their skin from sunburns.

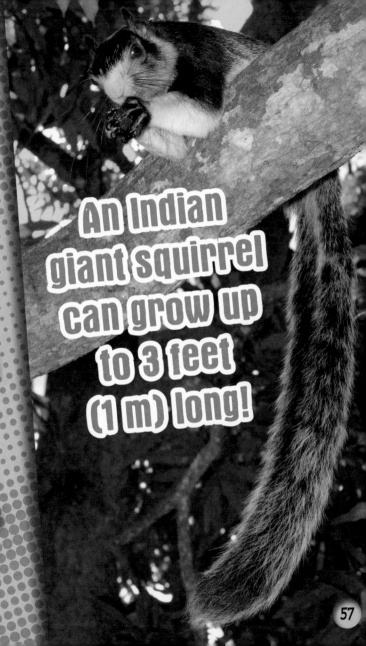

Humans are the only animals with a CHIN.

An Indian giant squirrel can grow up to 3 feet (1 m) long!

Inverloch Library in Victoria, Australia, has a surfboard that can be borrowed like a book!

Thought to be extinct, the tiny cave squeaker frog was sighted in 2017 for the first time in 55 years!

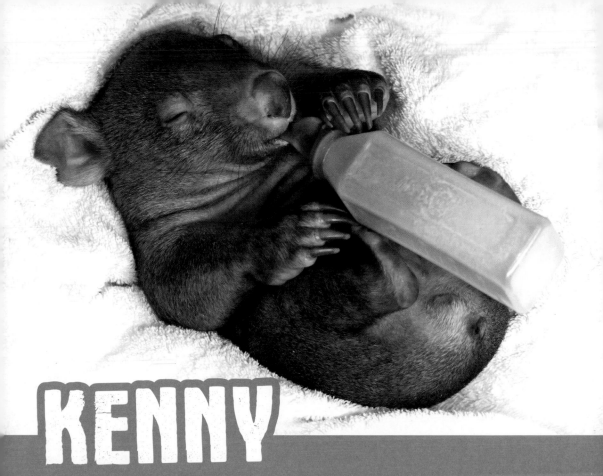

KENNY

the orphaned wombat at the Australian Reptile Park loves sleeping in drawers!

Orca pods are led by the oldest female in the group.

When this Yorkshire Terrier named

Goose

got a haircut, there was enough hair left over to create another dog!

Rhubarb can grow so fast you can hear it.

Banana ketchup is a popular condiment in the Philippines.

"Bird" used to be spelled B-R-I-D.

Gentoo penguins can swim at speeds of up to 22 miles per hour (35 kmph)!

Your right ear does a better job of listening to speech than your left.

Singaporeans are the fastest walkers in the world.

The *Apheloria virginiensis* millipede oozes a painful liquid that smells like **cherry soda.**

Japanese artist Masayoshi Matsumoto created these balloon animals without markers or tape—balloons only!

China chops down 20 million trees each year to make Chopsticks.

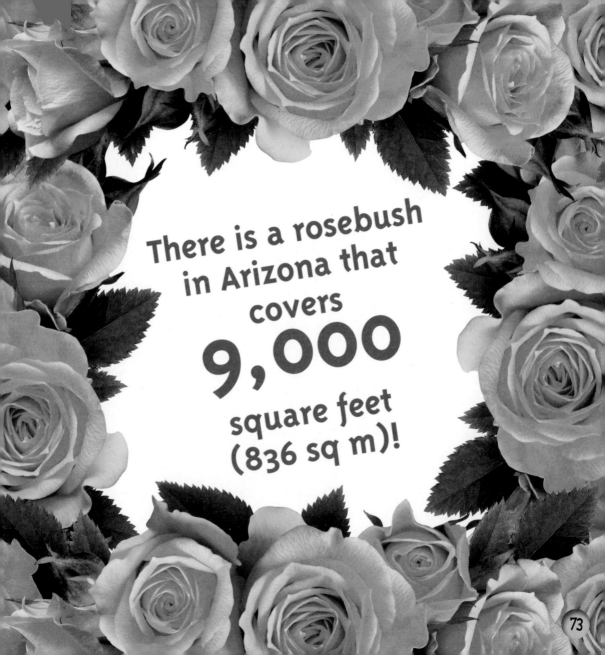

There is a rosebush in Arizona that covers **9,000** square feet (836 sq m)!

CHEETAH CUBS
have mohawk-like hair called **A MANTLE,** which may help them blend in with tall grass.

Falcons are more closely related to parrots than hawks or eagles.

Melbourne, Australia, was almost named "Batmania."

Oklahoma's official state vegetable is the watermelon. (Even though it's a fruit.)

Wavy Kelvin-Helmholtz clouds form

when close layers of wind are going different speeds.

A Danish jewelry-maker uses her

16 guinea pigs

to model her products!

Cornflakes have more genes than humans.

There were only about 20 SECONDS OF FUEL left when the Apollo 11 spacecraft landed on the Moon!

A baby cockroach is called a "nymph."

Ripe limes are yellow.

In 2012, scientists successfully grew a plant from a 32,000-year-old seed.

Helium has no effect on a frog's croak.

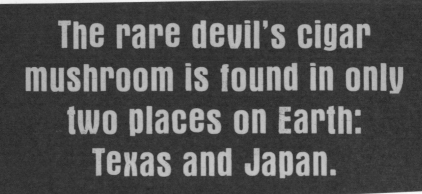

The rare devil's cigar mushroom is found in only two places on Earth: Texas and Japan.

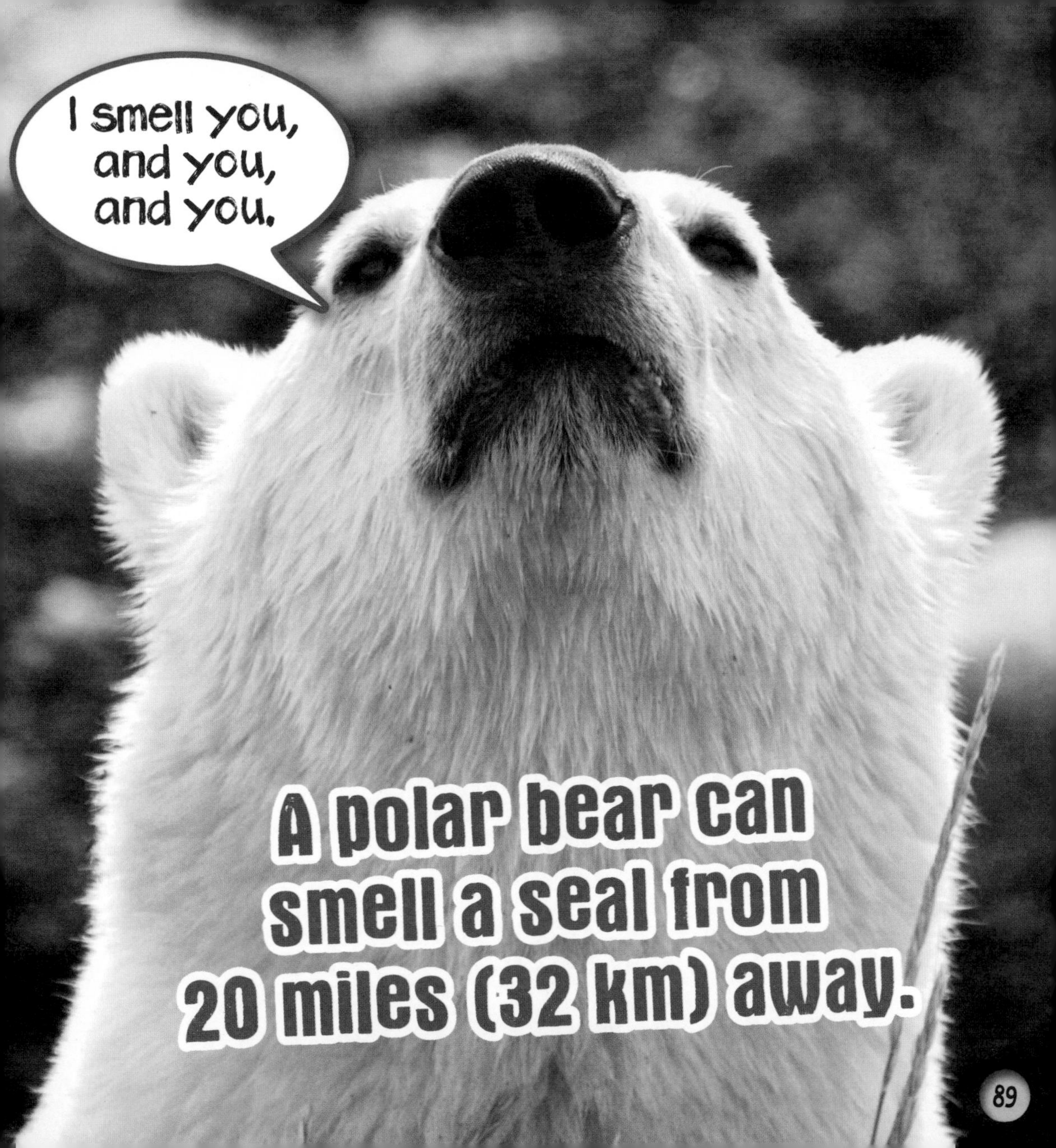

A polar bear can smell a seal from 20 miles (32 km) away.

In Los Angeles, residents can only have one rooster per household.

Call me later!

Albert Einstein hated wearing socks.

Herrings may communicate through farts.

SUNDEW

plants have sticky leaves for catching bugs.

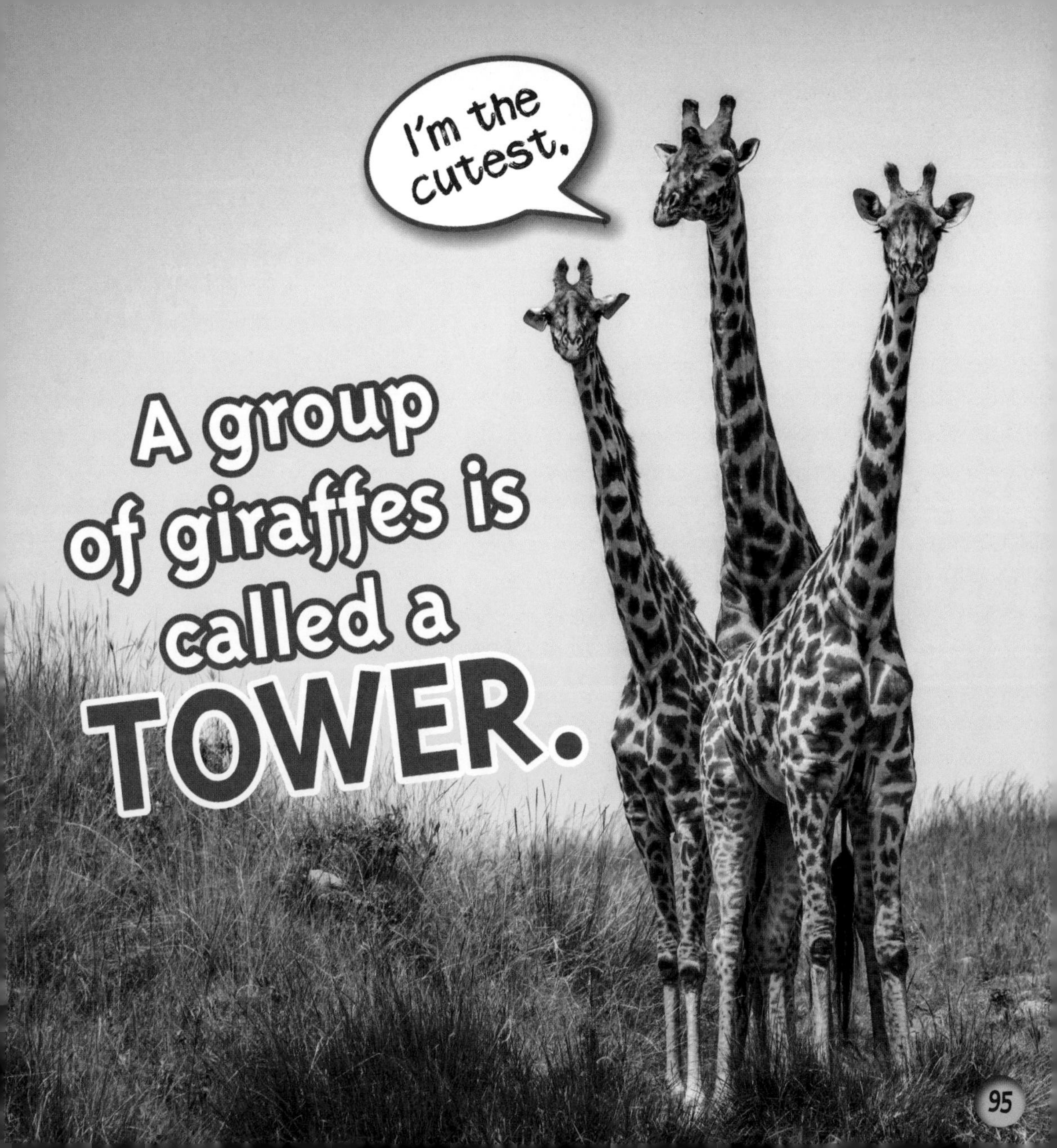

A group of giraffes is called a TOWER.

There are about
7,000,000,000,000,000,000,000,000,000
(7 octillion) atoms in
an adult human's body.

Cats have a
third eyelid.

Male Java sparrows tap their beaks on hard surfaces to add beats to their birdsongs.

The color of
dead leaves
is called
FILEMOT.

Ben & Jerry's
has an ice cream
GRAVEYARD.

OPI once created nail polish for dogs called PAWLISH!

They are PAW-rfect!

Believe it or not, this wild dog is actually a PAINTING done by South African artist Leon Fouche.

Photo: Ha...

A FROGFISH can suck up its prey in less than a second!

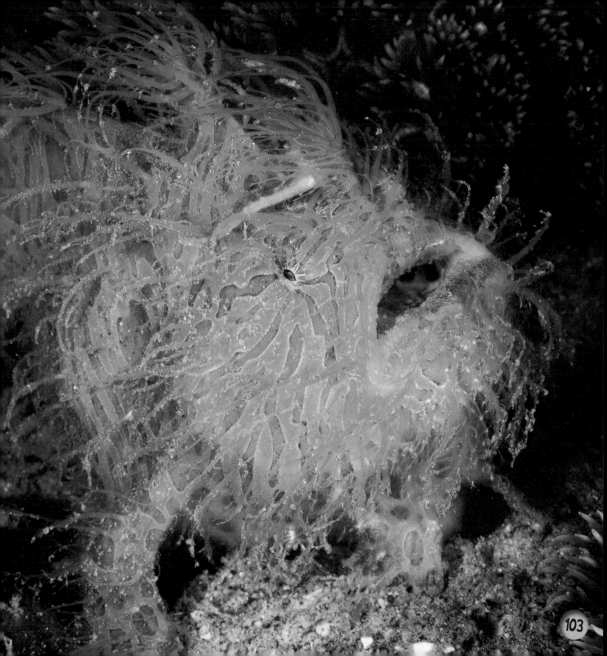

Shakespeare invented 1,700 words that we still use today.

The number is considered unlucky in Italy.

17

Yoda from *Star Wars* was originally going to be played by a monkey!

The Sun's core has a temperature of 27,000,000 °F (15,000,000 °C).

The Chinese giant salamander is the largest amphibian in the world— able to grow over 5 feet (1.5 m) long!

Teddy the cat looks just like **Dobby** from the *Harry Potter* series.

The lantern bug

uses its long nose to get through tree bark to the sap.

Indonesia is made-up of

over
13,000 islands.

HELLO
MY NAME IS

In 1991, a Swedish couple named their son Brfxxxccxxmnccclllmmnprxvclmnckssqlbb11116! They said it was pronounced

"Albin."

A group of porcupines is called a **PRICKLE.**

There are almost 20 million tons of gold in the world's oceans!

The Croatian Kuna is

the world's cleanest currency.

This hungry monkey in South Africa nabbed a family's breakfast as soon as their backs were turned!

Roller Coasters

The Smiler coaster at Alton Towers Resort in the U.K. has 14 LOOPS!

The first roller coasters were based on Russian ICE SLIDES.

The **CLICKING SOUND** of a roller coaster going uphill is made by a safety device.

A group of coaster fans once rode 74 different roller coasters in 10 U.S. states in just one day!

Silly String has been banned in the town of Southington, Connecticut since 1996.

Brazilian athletes funded their trip to the 1932 Olympics by selling coffee along the way.

118

Early bird gets the bone!

Bearded vultures eat mostly BONES.

Dogs
most likely dream about their owners.

Whole oranges float, but peeled oranges sink.

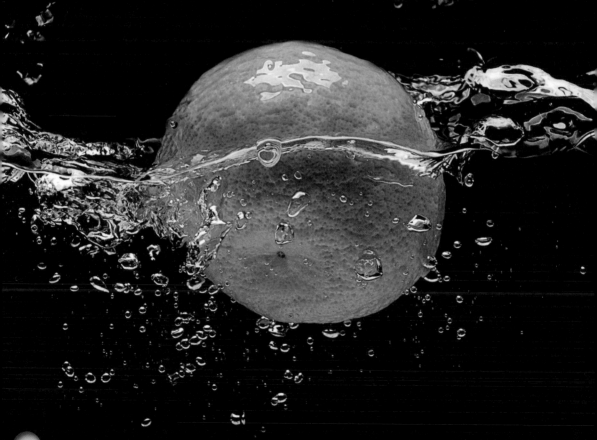

The band Coldplay was originally named "Starfish."

Some species of whales produce **blue-green milk**

123

Trompita the Elephant

She celebrated her 56ᵗʰ birthday at the Aurora Zoo in Guatemala with a fruit and veggie cake!

Those tiny pockets on blue jeans were originally used to hold pocket watches.

The spots on Lucy's ear

look like her own face!

Avocados

are berries.

Wyoming has only two sets of ESCALATORS.

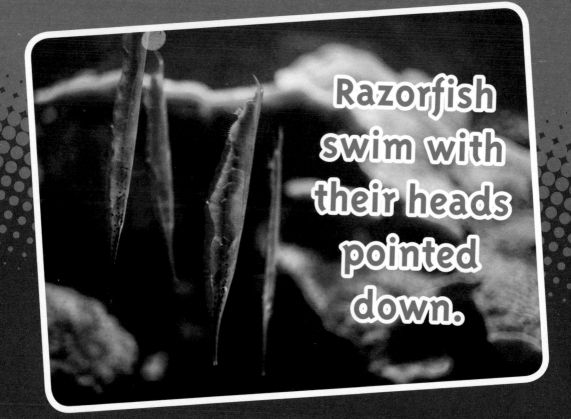

Razorfish swim with their heads pointed down.

There is an art scroll from Japan's Edo period depicting a **fart war.**

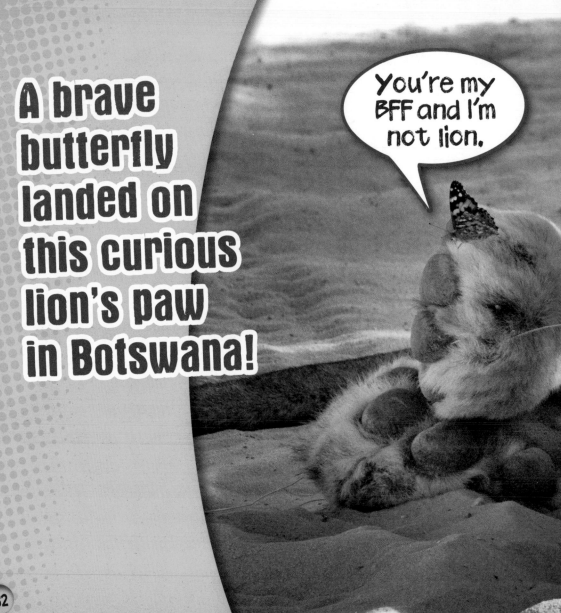

A brave butterfly landed on this curious lion's paw in Botswana!

You're my BFF and I'm not lion.

Iceland

Iceland's national dish is hákarl— fermented, rotted shark meat.

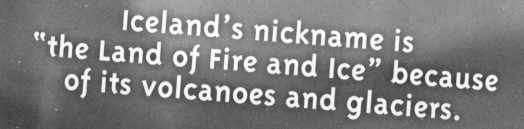

Iceland's nickname is "the Land of Fire and Ice" because of its volcanoes and glaciers.

Icelandic babies are left outside to nap in their strollers.

There are no mosquitoes in Iceland.

There's a town named "Cool" in California.

In Japan, 90 percent of mobile phones are waterproof because people use them even in the shower.

Most **BAT CALLS** are too high-pitched for humans to hear.

This rat snake found in Texas looks like it has a

MUSTACHE AND SUNGLASSES!

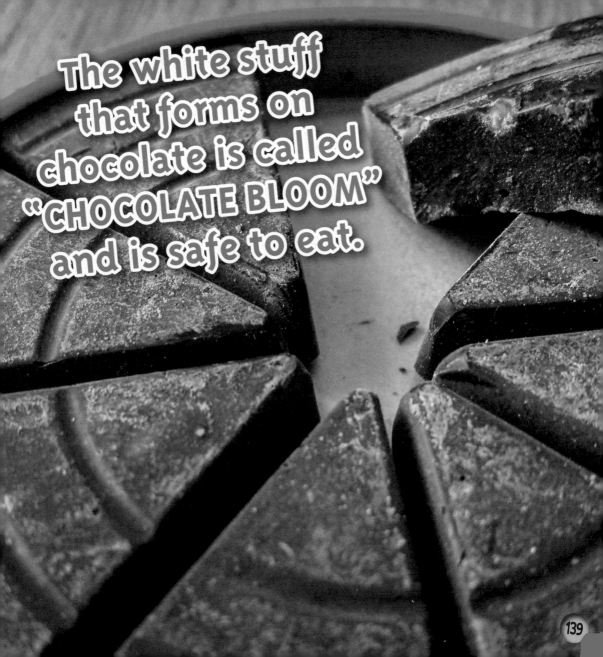

The white stuff that forms on chocolate is called "CHOCOLATE BLOOM" and is safe to eat.

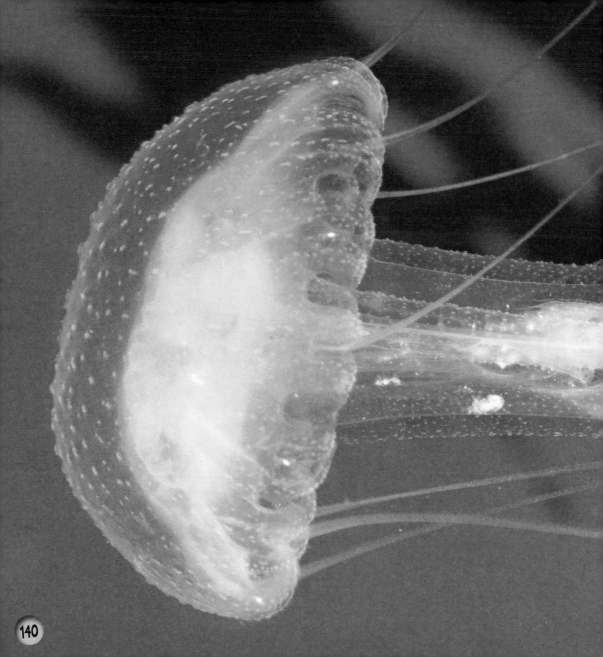

The Irish phrase for jellies, smugairle róin, means "SEAL SPIT."

Ships today have a higher chance of coming across an iceberg than the Titanic did.

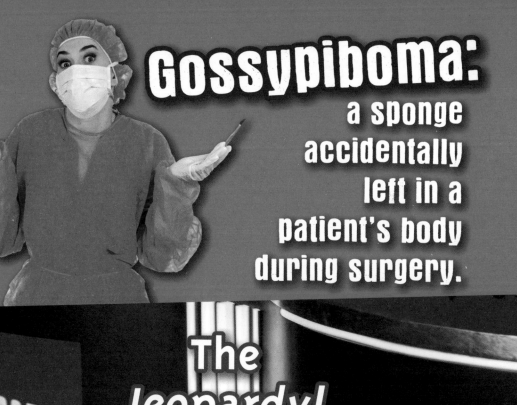

Gossypiboma: a sponge accidentally left in a patient's body during surgery.

The *Jeopardy!* theme song is named "Think!"

This cheetah

surprised this tourist on a safari in Kenya

when it jumped into the jeep!

I'm feeling gassy.

Cats are lactose intolerant.

146

The word sushi means sour rice, not raw fish.

Christmas was once ILLEGAL in the United States.

$$0 \times 9 + 1 = 1$$
$$1 \times 9 + 2 = 11$$
$$12 \times 9 + 3 = 111$$
$$123 \times 9 + 4 = 1{,}111$$
$$1{,}234 \times 9 + 5 = 11{,}111$$
$$12{,}345 \times 9 + 6 = 111{,}111$$
$$123{,}456 \times 9 + 7 = 1{,}111{,}111$$
$$1{,}234{,}567 \times 9 + 8 = 11{,}111{,}111$$
$$12{,}345{,}678 \times 9 + 9 = 111{,}111{,}111$$
$$123{,}456{,}789 \times 9 + 10 = 1{,}111{,}111{,}111$$

California sea lions can dive deeper than 900 feet (275 m) underwater!

Big Precious

the pig weighs over 1,300 pounds (590 kg) and carries her owner around town in China!

The word

T₁ **W**₄ **E**₁ **L**₁ **V**₄ **E**₁

is worth 12 points in Scrabble®.

Thomas Edison proposed to his wife in Morse code.

Some kangaroo species are almost always left-handed.

153

Hot chocolate tastes better in an ORANGE MUG.

There are 100 pounds (45 kg) of chocolate eaten every SECOND in the U.S.

The spa at the Hershey hotel in Pennsylvania offers whipped cocoa baths and chocolate skin treatments!

Sweet Chocolate Facts

It takes about 500 cocoa beans to make 1 pound (.5 kg) of chocolate!

Sound waves can be used to make things float in midair.

The word "usher" contains four pronouns—us, her, he, and she.

Goldfish can tell the difference between different **songs.**

157

Parrots

taste with the roof of their mouths.

Monastery Mutt

A monastery in Bolivia, adopted Carmelo, a stray dog, as its mascot.

His formal name is Friar Bigotón, or "Friar Mustache."

"Piranha" literally translates to
"TOOTH FISH"
in the Brazilian Tupí language.

There are approximately **1,200,000** rivets on the Golden Gate Bridge.

High heel shoes were originally worn by male soldiers.

Danniel the cow

is 6 ft 4 in (2 m) tall— almost 2 ft (0.6 m) taller than the average steer!

Vikings

Vikings landed in North America 500 years BEFORE COLUMBUS!

Viking men BLEACHED THEIR HAIR, possibly to get rid of LICE.

Vikings liked to stay clean and would use **TWEEZERS, COMBS,** and **EAR-CLEANERS.**

The offspring of a zebra and a donkey is

a zonkey!

168

Stinky garlic breath can be reduced by eating a raw apple.

Chewing gum can improve your memory.

The Hubble Space Telescope

can read newspaper print from a mile away!

Pooh the cat has titanium peg legs.

There is enough molten hot magma beneath Yellowstone National Park to fill the Grand Canyon 11 times.

Twelve-year-old Dawn Sciabica creates cute scenes with her pet ROACHES, BEETLES, and SNAILS!

Menu
Vanilla - 2$
Strawberry - 3$
chocolate - 3$
2 scoops - 5$
Sprinkles - 0.50 $

Male hooded seals have a large flab of skin on their heads that they can inflate!

Sand blown in from the Sahara desert fertilizes the Amazon rainforest.

The amount of concrete used to build the Hoover Dam would be enough to pave a road from California to New York.

A zoo in China angered visitors in 2013 when they tried to pass off a Tibetan mastiff dog as a lion.

A bookshop in Newtown, Australia, wraps books in plain paper to give readers a "blind date" with a book!

A photographer at an animal sanctuary in Indonesia posed this baby crocodile like a rock star.

Some penguins have brown feathers, rather than black, a rare condition called **ISABELLINISM.**

Less than 5 percent of the Earth's oceans have been explored.

Some spiders weave zigzag patterns

into their webs!

Adult cats don't meow to each other— just to humans!

Feed me!

Air pollution in China increases snowfall in California.

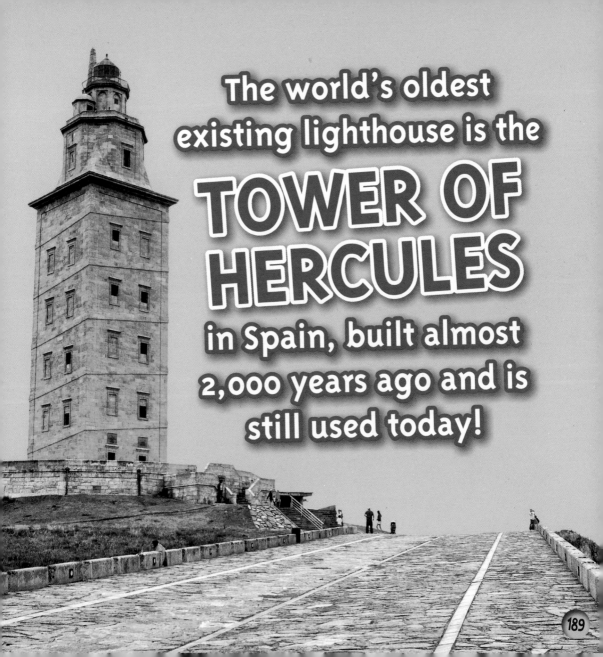

The world's oldest existing lighthouse is the

TOWER OF HERCULES

in Spain, built almost 2,000 years ago and is still used today!

189

Manatees
have smooth brains.

The U.S. flags on the Moon have turned white.

The Irish Wolfhound is the tallest dog breed in the world!

Abraham Lincoln

Abraham Lincoln was the first president to appear on a U.S. coin.

At 6 feet 4 inches (2 m), Lincoln was the tallest U.S. president.

"Honest Abe" was the first U.S. president to sport a full beard.

The 16th president was an accomplished wrestler, having only one recorded loss.

Denmark is the only other country 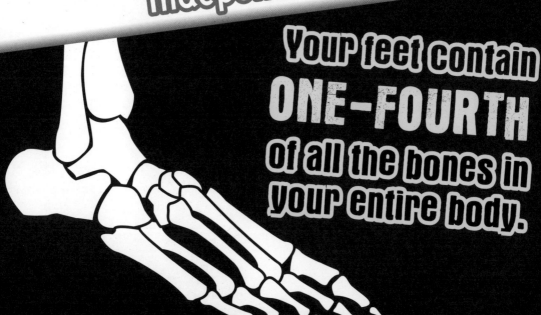 to celebrate the United States' Independence Day.

Your feet contain **ONE-FOURTH** of all the bones in your entire body.

KOALAS

will hug trees to cool down.

Wisconsin is the first U.S. state to have an official microbe—the cheese-producing bacterium *Lactococcus lactis*.

Star flowers smell like DEAD FISH.

This strange **TWO-HEADED** creature is actually two camels standing next to each other in India.

People used to believe witches would use tomatoes to turn people into

WEREWOLVES!

Steve Jobs had a mild fear of buttons.

There is a type of frog that gets smaller as it grows from tadpole to frog.

Guru,
a chimp living at Mysore Zoo in India, **LOST ALL OF HIS HAIR** due to a condition called alopecia.

Americans eat over **20 million** hot dogs at baseball games every year!

O.M.G. was first used over 100 years ago.

209

Otters juggle rocks!

Food must be mixed with saliva for your tongue to be able taste it.

Zebras cause more injuries to U.S. zookeepers than any other animal.

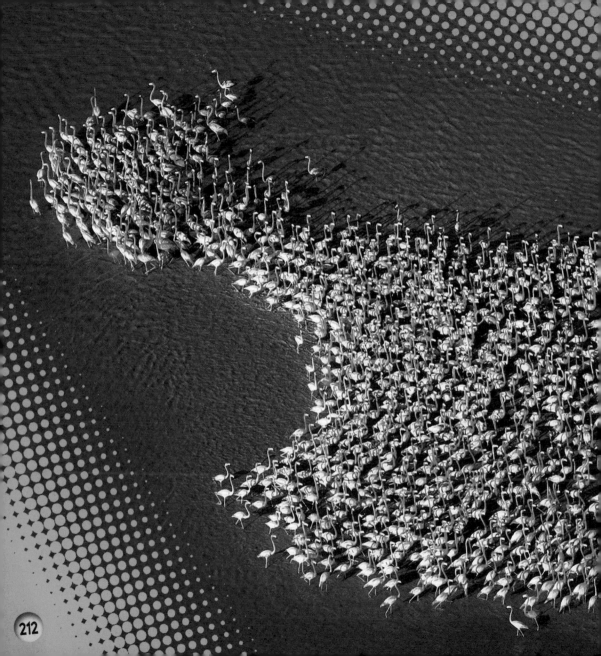

These flamingos in Mexico were caught forming the shape of a **giant flamingo!**

Shakespeare had pierced ears.

A cat's purr can help heal injuries.

There is a rare disease that makes a person's urine smell like **MAPLE SYRUP.**

Strong winds cause the water of Waipuhia Falls in Hawaii to flow UP!

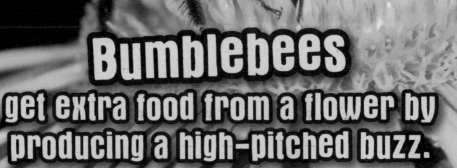

Bumblebees
get extra food from a flower by producing a high-pitched buzz.

The patent
for the
FIRE HYDRANT
was lost
IN A FIRE.

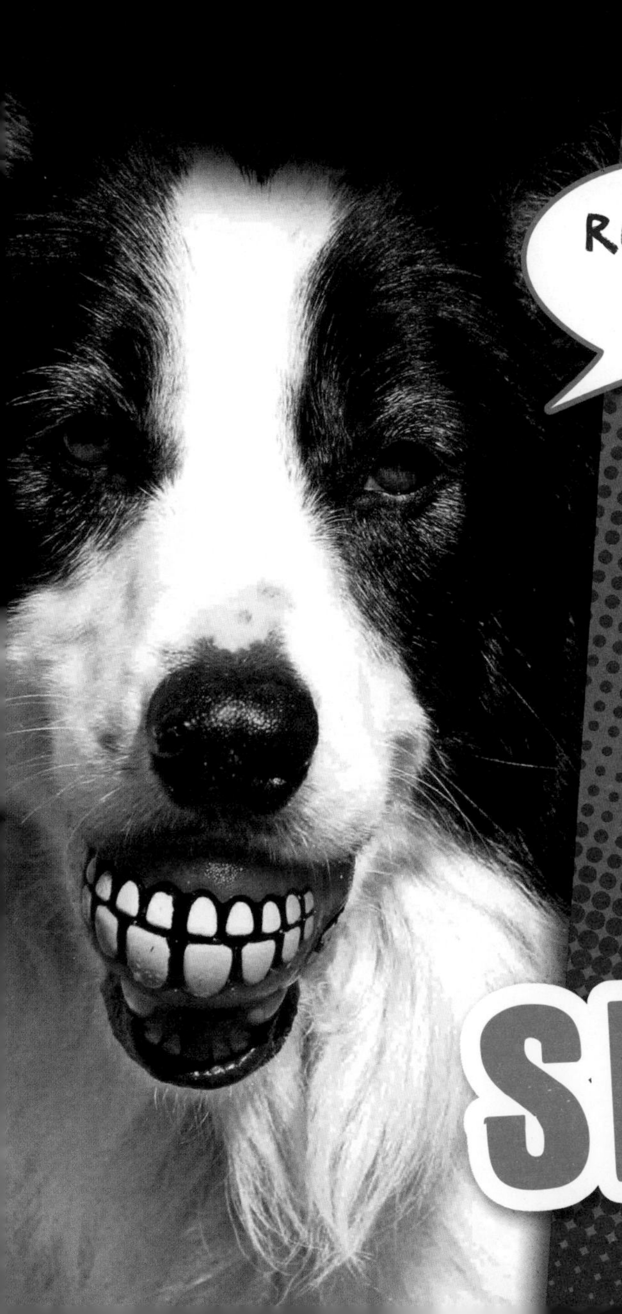

The Rogz Grinz ball gives any dog a big, toothy

smile!

INDEX

PHOTO CREDITS

Have you seen books one, two, three, four, and five? They're packed with even more fun facts and silly stories!

we hope you enjoyed the book!

If you have a fun fact or silly story, why not email us at bionresearch@ripleys.com or write to us at BION Research, Ripley Entertainment Inc., 7576 Kingspointe Parkway, Suite 188, Orlando, Florida 32819, U.S.A.